EXTREME SELLING

(How to be an all-star sales rep in your organization.)

Jeffrey Carr

Chapter Outlines

Introduction

Section 1: Prospecting

Chapter 1 – Customer Profile

Chapter 2 – Local Profile

Chapter 3 – Target Market

Chapter 4 – Techniques

Chapter 5 – Execution

Section 2: Relationships

Chapter 6 – Establishing a Basic Relationship

Chapter 7 – Building Trust

Chapter 8 – Creating Needs/Wants

Chapter 9 – Project Team

Chapter 10 – Matching Services with Needs/Wants

Chapter 11 – Trial Balloon

Section 3: Proposals

Chapter 12 – Review Timeline

Chapter 13 – Review Needs/Wants

Chapter 14 – Match Services with Needs/Wants

Chapter 15 – Provide Excellent ROI

Chapter 16 – Close by Securing Dates for Installation/Delivery

Chapter 17 – Sign Contracts

Section 4: After the Sale

Chapter 18 – Push for Quick Installation/Delivery

Chapter 19 – Be Present with Customer to Showcase Services

Chapter 20 – Thank Customer for Business and Start Discussions for Phase II

Section 5: Additional Activities

Chapter 21 – Branding

Chapter 22 – Networking

Chapter 23 – Social Media

Conclusion

INTRODUCTION

I never had a plan to get into sales. I did have a plan to get out of retail management. And then I interviewed for a position in sales with Monroe Systems for Business, a subsidiary of Litton Industries, and all that changed.

This guy I was interviewing with told me that if I did what he told me to do, I would make a lot of money. So I accepted his offer on the spot. I went home and told my wife that I was leaving my $14,000 a year job in retail for a $12,000 a year job in outside sales. I also told her that this guy said he could teach me how to make money. (Lesson #1 – you gotta take some risks to make money).

That was the day that my life changed.

I loved the thrill of competition and comradery with the other sales reps, as my boss used to post our percentage of quota on the back wall every week of the quota month, with the promise that whoever finished last at the end of the month would be fired. I also loved the fact that the harder (or sometimes luckier) I worked, the more money I made.

Within a year, Litton sold Monroe to some guy with a little bit of credit, but no idea how to run a sales organization, and we were put on straight commission. (Lesson #2 – Don't work for free, and don't work for a loser). I next landed a job with Honeywell Inc., selling parts for heating systems.

I found out early on that guys would come in asking for Honeywell parts from different divisions, parts my division did not make. I also found out that I could do an interoffice transfer and get those parts. At that point my new motto was," If it says Honeywell, you can buy it here". That went great until my boss got a call from a VP in the industrial division, letting him know that I had sold more industrial parts than all of the industrial division in the state of Ohio, and they were not happy, because I was in the Building Control Division. Fortunately, my boss told me to keep doing what I was doing, and in less than six months, I was the top inside sales person in the organization, with branches throughout the US.

At that point, my boss asked me if I would be interested in going into outside sales. I told him that I did not think so, because I noticed that 90 percent of the outside reps did not make it one year. He advised me to give it a try.

I did give it a try, with flipcharts, brochures, scripts, formal training, everything the company told me to use. The only problem was - I was terrible! My appointments turned into site surveys, and my surveys turned into proposals, and my proposals turned into nothing.

At that point my sales manager asked to ride along with me one day to see what might be the problem. We went to the first appointment, and I did everything my training told me to do. My prospect's brother was a competitor of mine, but I pushed forward setting up a site visit and time for a proposal. After the meeting, my manager suggested we get some coffee. He proceeded to tell me that this had been the worst sales call he had ever been on. He asked me what I thought our chances were of getting some business from this prospect. I told him that I thought it was pretty good. He asked me if I really thought that this guy would fire the company that his brother owned and hire us, especially since I had not uncovered any issues with his current service. Since he was local, our price would also be at least double what he was currently paying. I responded that according to the training I had received, I was confident that we could get this business.

At this point, my manager explained to me that all of the brochures and flipcharts and action plans and training were designed to help the average person survive for a year or maybe two in sales, but they were definitely not designed to produce a successful, winning sales career.

My manager then told me to use the product knowledge that I had been given and have a conversation with the prospect at our next appointment. I sold that next prospect a comprehensive package of goods and services for all of his facilities.

That was the day that I realized that I had to get a lot smarter about how sales works and how to convert my efforts into high sales productivity. Companies and their training departments do not know how to sell. They know how to create activity, but that's all (Lesson #3).

From that moment, I spent the next thirty years trying to create the optimal sales formula. I can honestly tell you that I have created that formula. I know this because within two years at Honeywell, I was the Number 1 or 2 sales rep within the company each year, while also achieving above average profits and a 95% close rate.

I left Honeywell in 1993 to start my own business, competing with my former employer. My startup company was booking more new business in the Ohio school building retrofit market, with just me as the sales department, than my two closest competitors, both Fortune 100 companies with large sales forces.

Well, maybe I was lucky. Maybe I had the good customers, or the cheapest prices, or who knows what.

I left sales and went into teaching at the college level. Everything was great until we decided to move our family from Ohio to North Carolina. I could not get a teaching job that paid my bills. So I decided at the age of 51 to go back into sales for a living.

I was hired by ADT to work in their commercial security business. I started with no customers and a territory that was mostly rural. I was in a new area where I did not know a soul, in an economic market very different from Northeastern Ohio. My manager told me that their average close rate was 30%, and that the goal was to throw as many quotes out there as possible, hoping some may turn into orders.

I started in May 2012. I implemented the formula in this book and made President's Club in 2013, my first full year with the company. In 2014, I finished Number 1 in sales in the company, with one of the highest profit margins in the organization. I was Number 6 in the company in 2015 when I left sales to go into college teaching full-time so I could write this book. During this short time, I had brought in two of the largest customers in the entire organization, all while dealing with a sell-off of our residential business and the name ADT, operations change-ups and layoffs that affected our installation and service capabilities, and a management structure that disagreed with just about every strategy and tactic I employed.

So if you want to ask me if I know how to go from nothing to the top of a sales organization, I think I have proven that I do. I also did all of this without sacrificing my family commitments or my health.

If you truly want to be the best in your company, your industry, your city and state, EXTREME SELLING will get you there if you employ the strategies without fail exactly as they are laid out in this book. One warning: if you cut corners, it won't work.

HAPPY SELLING!

I dedicate this book to the three best salespeople I have ever met:

Chet Embley for teaching me how to sell,

Duane Shover for teaching me how to work with people,

And most of all,

My wonderful wife Kaylie Carr for teaching me that whenever things look bleak, just sell more.

TERMS YOU WILL NEED TO KNOW:

Suspect: Organization that fits your basic customer profile or target market. You have not met with them yet.

Prospect: Organization that you have met with, talked about their needs, decided that this group can and will buy from you if you offer the right solutions.

Sponsor: Your lead individual at the prospect's organization. They are at all of the meetings. They help you get access to info and people you need to meet with. They keep the decision maker involved in the process. They get decision maker approvals along the way.

Detractor: Does not want you or your company there. They may not like you, your company, or your ideas. Or as one detractor once told me, "They take me to the Kentucky Derby every year, you don't).

Decision Maker: The person or group that ultimately makes the decision on doing business with you.

Approvers: People that you need to have on board in the organization that cannot say yes to hire you, but can say no and keep you out if you do not address their concerns along the way.

Sales/Branch Manager: Person who probably hired you, sends you to training, and wants to talk about your pipeline and how big it is, and has as many meetings as possible each day instead of helping you learn the sales process and how to maximize your sales. May not want you to sell a lot – will just make his/her quota go up next year and has a maximum limit on commissions. As a result, likes a lot of little sales, not big ones.

Regional Manager: The person that probably cares that you are bringing in huge accounts.

Operations Team: The group that has to install and service what you sell. They can make or break your success.

Section 1: Prospecting

Chapter 1 – Customer Profile

The first thing you have to figure out is who is going to buy from you. Unfortunately, and in contrast with what your sales manager tells you, not everyone is a potential customer. There are three types of prospects – those that need what you sell and have the ability to buy it, those that may buy from you, and those that will never buy from you.

We want to identify those in the first category. Those in the second category are fine for a warm sunny day when you don't have any appointments and feel like talking to someone new. Those in the third category are not ones that you should visit, talk to, or think about.

So, who are the prospects in this first category? I don't know. They are different for each of you, but I can tell you how to figure it out.

You have to put together a list of the type of customers that will buy often and a lot. There are several ways to do this.

1) Who buys from your company now? Talk to the other reps in the office. Ask them who some of their customers are. What industries are they in? How much do they buy? How often do they buy? Go to your company's website. What types of customers are featured there. All of these inquiries will lead to the biggest and most frequent customers that are currently buying from your company.
2) Who is buying from your competitors? Again, go to their website and see who they are selling to. Companies all love to brag about who they are selling to and for how much. Use this info to start putting together a list of who may buy from you.
3) What kind of organizations might need what you sell? Just take some time and think about what industries would be good candidates for your products and services. Where do you see examples of companies currently using what you sell?

4) Listen to everything you hear in the office. Which type of customers seem to be problems? Who are the biggest customers in your office long-term? What do they say about other offices? Listen to regional managers and sales reps from other offices – who are they selling to?

Take all of this information and start to compile a list of typical customers for your company. When I first started in sales, I was selling office equipment. In talking with our sales manager, I found out that companies with large accounting departments bought a lot of business calculators and copiers, and small companies bought our more expensive magnetic-strip accounting machines.

I realized that I had to sell about 30 calculators per month to make my quota. I also realized that I had to sell one accounting machine or copier to make my quota. It also occurred to me that everyone in my business was calling on large customers. Nobody was calling on small businesses. Let's see – I could make thirty sales in a very competitive market or one sale in a non-competitive market to make my quota. Gee, that seems like a simple decision. I started spending all of my time marketing account machines to small business. (Forget copiers – we had an inferior product in a market where five copier sales reps a day were walking into every business). While marketing accounting machines, some customers would also buy a couple of calculators or a copier now and then.

Also, accounting machines needed supplies that could only be purchased through my company – repeat business.

It gets better – this was a time when computers were just coming out, and older business owners were fighting the new technology. Add that to the list. I called on old, family-owned businesses run by first or second generation owners that would buy an accounting machine to make their life easier and let the world know that they did not need a computer.

OK, so what do we have so far? We have old businesses run by the founders or family. Who would this include?

Hardware stores

Oil delivery businesses

Large family farms

Heating and A/C service providers

Plumbing companies

Any small business using credit with the same customers each month

Lumber yards

Produce suppliers

This list could go on and on. These are the people buying what I am selling, but nobody else is calling on them because they are too small and antiquated to buy our products. Ha! These are exactly who bought from me. I only needed one sale per month to make quota, save my job, and pay my bills. If I happened to sell two in a month, great! (Also, small business owners talk to each other).

Ok, you say, I got lucky with this one. Well, maybe. Let's see how this worked with my next position.

I'm hired to sell heating and air conditioning contracts for businesses. By the way, at this point, I have no idea how heating and air conditioning works. I find out from the other reps that we are by far the most expensive in the industry. So, I am supposed to sell something I know nothing about and charge twice as much as everyone else. Great.

So, here's what I do. I watch these two guys in our office that seem to be the superstars. They are selling everything. Nobody else is selling anything. Who are their customers? Schools and government. They are fixing up old school and public buildings and then putting long-term maintenance agreements on the buildings. They are promising to save the customer money by fixing up their heating systems, causing them to run more efficiently.

I also read the weekly, monthly, and quarterly newsletters sent out by the company. They are bragging about the same thing – selling these big fixup projects with long-term maintenance projects. They are also getting a lot of repeat business from these same customers because they have a number of facilities in the area.

I find out that the guys getting all of the business are the only ones allowed to call on schools or governments, and we also have a rep that calls on all of the hospitals. That leaves me with nothing. My options are to quit or outsmart the system. I choose the latter. I look at my territory (which I am given because the last two guys that had it were fired for non-performance, so nobody else wants it), and I realize that I have to figure out what other types of businesses have the same buying style as the schools, government, hospitals, etc.

What did these businesses have in common that made them such good prospects? They each had multiple locations and served the public. OK, now who else fits that profile?

Retail with multiple locations

Banks

Well, that is about all. I made a list of all of the non-national businesses in my territory that fit that profile. It was not a long list, but it was a start. Most of these were in the county with the largest city, Canton, OH, so that is where I went.

Every day, I went into the office, planned my day and headed for Canton. I mailed letters to these prospects at their corporate office and then scheduled to stop in at each location. On the way, I would stop in at other businesses along the way, just to be sure I did not pass up any opportunities that did not fit my profile.

The result is that within the first year, I sold a major automation system with maintenance to a four-store retail provider, as well as smaller individual contracts with a number of the local banks in the area. This was enough to exceed my quarterly quotas and pay my bills (plus a little extra now and then). I never did get great at selling to banks corporately. I guess there was just something about my personality and selling style that did not match their buying habits.

When I went back into sales in 2012 at the age of 51, I employed the same strategy. It appeared to me that ADT's success was based on selling cameras to customers that needed a large number of cameras for customer safety as well as surveillance. Their largest customer was a hospital with multiple locations. This meant that my potential customer was going to be building owners that had multiple facilities and a large cost if there were losses or injuries at their locations, especially if there were large scale injuries or an intruder determined to cause problems.

I started calling on this type of prospect with some success. Our office was located in Raleigh, NC, but I had the only territory with no real part of the city. Except for one little sliver. It just so happened that on that small sliver of land was a very old, private university – Shaw University. They did not have many remote locations, but they did have multiple buildings on the campus. More about them later.

In the meantime, I sold some little systems and learned a little bit about commercial security, building a small base of references for when I would need them.

In each case, I worked diligently but quickly to assemble a profile of what type of business would be most likely to buy and buy repeatedly based on what I saw my company's top reps doing, what my competitors were doing, and the talk in the office. You have to be able to answer the question, "Who is going to buy from me?" before you really start making your move to the top.

KEY POINT: YOU CANNOT RELY ON YOUR SALES TRAINING TO BE SUCCESSFUL. THEIR TRAINING HAS A SUCCESS RATE OF ABOUT 10% AT BEST.

Chapter 2 – Local Profile

Let's start with the talk in the office. Your office may have a different customer profile than another office. This could be for a variety of reasons. In North Carolina, we have the mountains, Raleigh, rural NC, Charlotte, and the beach. Each of these has very different buying patterns. When I worked in the Midwest, every area had similar buying patterns, regardless of the demographics.

Depending on where you are located, you need to factor your prospect profile with your local profile. Raleigh, NC is a wonderful place to sell, primarily because the people and businesses are progressive in their desire to maximize their resources and experience for their customers. This tends to make them open to new ideas and tactics to achieve their strategies. However, it is a very different profile from Akron, Ohio.

Knowing the nuances in the sales cycles of your individual areas is vital to executing this process successfully. This book is not designed to explain how to sell in your city, but once you know the strategies for success, you can apply them to the local business culture.

The local profile is designed by taking everything we discussed in Chapter 1 and applying to your local area. This includes taking the successful customer profile nationally and applying it based on what the reps in your office are doing. In Ohio, we had a large number of buildings built before 1930. The companies were also very old. In Raleigh, I have found very few old buildings, and those that are, are actually older yet better maintained than the ones in Akron. This forces the reps to utilize different tactics. For example, a major concern of building managers and owners in Ohio was that the buildings were uncomfortable for employees. Old heating systems led to freezing areas as well as overheating, causing windows to be open in January when the outside temperature was well below freezing. In NC, there was very little concern over uncomfortable conditions. Instead the focus was on automation for efficiency and a good working environment for employees, visitors, and customers.

The overall customer profile is still the same, but the reasons behind their needs and wants were somewhat different, and as such they required a slightly different approach.

KEY POINT: YOU HAVE TO KNOW HOW AND WHY THE CUSTOMERS IN YOUR AREA BUY OR YOU WILL NEVER BE SUCCESSFUL.

Chapter 3 – Target Market

Now that we have established who is going to buy from us and adapted our probable customer profile to meet the needs of the local market, we can assemble and revise our target market. This may seem simple, but in most instances, this is never done. Failure to know your target market will doom your chances of extreme levels of success.

You also cannot rely on your employer to provide you with a profile of your target market. At one point during my tenure with ADT/Tyco, some marketing execs game to our office to educate us on the marketing of our products. When they were done with their presentation (Did I mention that I hate in-house meetings – I never sold an extra dollar because of something the company told me during a meeting), they asked if there were any questions. After a few softballs, I asked who our target market was. They asked me to explain what I meant. I said, you know, who buy our products? What type of business is our typical and most repetitive buyer? Their answer was, "I don't know that we have ever thought about that – maybe it is something we should look into".

It is no wonder that most of the products being introduced did not complement each other and did not fit any type of customer. Each time a new product or service was introduced, it had nothing in common with the last or next product. It was obvious that they had no idea who their target market was.

Ok, so here is what you need to do. This is VERY IMPORTANT!!! I hate to have to yell, but this is the key to everything else.

1. What industry seems to be the largest purchaser of your company's products and services?
2. Who is second and third?

Go ahead – write it down with as much detail as possible. What I am looking for here is K-12 education, hospitals, government, small businesses, large businesses, colleges, etc. From the marketing crap put out by your company, where do the big buyers come from?

3. Who are the five biggest customers in your office? What industries are they in?
4. OK, now combine all of this info, and write it down. Now.
5. Now list the categories #1, #2, #3.
6. Who is #1? That is where we want to spend a very significant part of our prospecting. If it is hospitals, they are our primary target market. If next is small businesses in rural areas, they are our secondary market.
7. A target market can have many pieces, such as historically black universities in an urban setting, with a lot of older buildings, yet receiving federal grants each year. In my area, that is a very narrow, yet productive market. If you only have two or three of these, yet they each yield $100,000 in revenue for you each year, against a sales quota of $300,000 per year, that's a nice position to be in with only two customers.

If you haven't realized it yet, what we are trying to do here is make the most money with the least effort. Why spend all your time cold calling supermarkets if your company has not sold any large projects to a supermarket nationally or locally in the last two years. You would be better off going home and mowing your yard – you would be more productive that way.

You may be able to create a new market by looking at the attributes of an existing target market by applying those attributes to a potential lucrative non-market. For instance, our target market at ADT/Tyco was hospitals. This was where the big money was being made. These were the largest customers nationally as well as locally. What are the characteristics of a hospital? Large buildings, critical issues, multiple sites. Who else has these same criteria? How about universities and housing units. It is possible that I could use the needs and benefits of hospitals and apply them to these other two areas where we were getting little or no business.

KEY POINT: YOU HAVE TO KNOW PRECISELY WHO IS GOING TO BUY FROM YOU TO BE SUCCESSFUL.

Chapter 4 – Techniques

As in any endeavor, there is more than one way to interact with suspects to convert them to prospects and then convert them into customers or clients. This chapter will look at some of these methods, with limited analysis, in an effort to encourage you to try each of these and determine which methods are most applicable to your situation. All of these situations are determinant on what type of customer they may be. In this book, I am typically referring to a B2B suspect. B2C suspects (private, individual consumers) have different buying and selling habits. Our discussion throughout will be for B2B sales, however, most of these ideas can be adapted to B2C with little change or effort.

The oldest tried-and-true method is to utilize the US postal service. For decades in the U.S., sales people have sent mailers or flyers to suspects (A suspect is someone that you think might do business with you based on some feature that they have that makes you think they would be a good candidate for your products and services). These suspects are typically from a list that you have composed based on some characteristic of that suspect. This list typically contains some suspects that will never buy from you, but you do not know this yet. It will take a little bit more work to see what type of suspect we have.

The mailer is typically generic in its presentation, as you are not sure of the buying characteristics of those who will be receiving your mailer. At this point, all you have is a list with some characteristic that may fit your customer profile. It is also a fairly inexpensive way to reach suspects, as well as a method of contact that is not very time consuming. Unfortunately, it is also not very effective.

When I first started out, direct mail was not a bad way to prospect. I would try and send out 10 letters a day, which typically took less than one half hour each day. It could be done in the office before leaving on appointments all day and before customer or prospects were ready to see reps. I got one new prospect every couple of weeks, so it was worthwhile. Add this to other means of prospecting, and it could add an extra sale or two each month.

Typically, these mailers were geared to areas or types of suspects where we or I had been successful. Mailers were typically for higher priced products, so it was conceivable that you could meet your quota each month just off of mailers. If someone called in off of a mailer, they were probably a serious buyer. I got some great accounts from flyers.

Unfortunately, at the time, the response rate for mailers was 1-3%. That is about the lowest success rate of any type of commercial prospecting. I am sure that this percentage has gone down significantly throughout the past two decades as computers and phones have changed how we do business.

Another way to prospect is to drop off info and your business card as you drive around in your territory. I have known a couple of people that have done this as a regular part of their prospecting. One was my first manager, who thought this was a great way to prospect. I don't know why, but I never made one dollar prospecting this way. I guess with a lot of follow-up, these can be converted into prospects, but in my case, even though I really tried to make this work, it was like throwing my time and resources into the trash.

Times change, and various parts of the country do business differently, but I used to have a lot of luck researching a company and then calling a top executive to set an appointment. In recent years, however, this has gotten very difficult. People have administrative assistants, do not answer their phones or return messages, and have two or three barriers to entry, physical or human. This technique may work very well for you, and I would still use it if this is your best avenue of access to the person you would like to meet with. It may require some creativity to get through to your suspect. Leaving messages with an assistant or voicemail may not get you a return call.

Most reps will tell you that they hate cold calling. But those that are proficient at it will tell you that it can be the most valuable type of prospecting on the planet. It does not take innate skill or wisdom, but it does take practice. You have to develop some sort of routine that creates a quick basis of rapport that allows you to get past the gatekeeper and engage the target.

I have found that this method works well with a non-aggressive approach. Typically, this method may include asking a few benign questions that get the gatekeeper to see you as person, not a sales rep. They see those all of the time and consider them to be somewhat of a nuisance with no value to the company. They see their primary focus as one that ensures that you do not get to see your target. Letting you in is a failure that their boss will not like.

Your inquiries have to be very conversational to work. I would not start with, "What do you guys do here?", but instead would focus more on asking to see the target. That can turn into a discussion that starts with, "Maybe you can help me. Who is responsible for making sure that everyone here stays safe, you know, makes sure that nobody meaning to do harm gets in?". The person that you are talking to wants to be safe and does not want any "bad" people getting in because they may be the first to be shot. This tends to motivate them to get you in to see the person responsible for making these decisions. Now you are not a nuisance, she thinks you are there to save her life. Again, there is a fine line in using this method, but when deployed properly, it works very well in getting you in and getting you to the highest level, right person.

Some sales people are lucky enough to get leads or referrals. Most of my career, I have not gotten referrals. I may have a prospect call or email a current customer, but I found that getting referrals in the commercial sales market typically did not work well. Again, we would sometimes get testimonials for our portfolio but not really referrals as such.

One area that does work very effectively, especially for new reps, is to call on existing customers. Even if they hate your company, there is a possibility for a sale. If they love the company, this is an opportunity to show that you care as their rep as well as, in many cases, sell them additional products or just sell them updated products for their system. If they hate you and the company, this is an opportunity to fix their problems and maybe sell them various items to make their system work better. Either way, I would seriously incorporate this into your sales system, as it can be a significant provider of sales. It also gives you at least one appointment to start each day if needed. As a new rep, you will also learn a lot about your company and how it works, as well as what customers are looking for from you and the company.

In one position I did occasionally get leads. Most of them were not qualified, and as such, they should not have been called leads. They should have been called, "if you have nothing else to do, maybe you should stop here and try to convince these people that they called or emailed your company.

I did get one lead that paid off huge for the company and me. I would like to tell you that I made the initial call on this customer, but I did not. They happened to call our office one day, stating that they would like to buy one panic button. The sales manager figured that this was a $50 sale that I could probably handle, so he sent me an email with the particulars.

My manager told me to meet with the VP of Operations. I tried to make an appointment, but he seemed to be busy regardless of what day I wanted to schedule to meet. After ten minutes of dancing with him on the phone, I said," How about if I stop by around 9:00 tomorrow, take a look at where you guys want this button, and talk with you if you are free". He said OK. The next morning I arrive at the campus at ask to see the VP. Of course, he was too busy to talk with me, even for a few minutes. I asked his assistant if she had any idea what he was looking for. She told me that the President of the University had received some death threats and wanted a way to signal security in case somebody showed up that meant harm to her. I was new, but I did know that this button would need to tie into some type of system to alert campus police, and that she would probably be dead by the time campus police were able to respond.

I asked the assistant if I could speak with campus police as to how we would signal them in the case of a threat. Now again, I am looking at a $50 sale, but being new, I had plenty of time on my hands. This was a Thursday morning, and I did not have much else to do Thurs. or Fri., and I was leaving for training on Monday, so I decided to poke around a bit.

The assistant called the campus Chief of Police and told him that I would be coming over to talk with him about this panic button. As it turned out, he was a very nice guy who said, "Sure, send him over". I walked over to the campus police office and told the Chief why I was there. He was aware of the situation and asked me to sit and talk about it with him. I mentioned some of the disadvantages of a button, such as the fact that the perpetrator could probably get in, kill the victim, and get out before anyone could get to her, assuming she could even get to the button. He agreed that this may not be the best scenario. So what do I do? I have a nice guy in what appears to be a decision-making position, agreeing that we may need to look at another option, with an organization that probably has the money to spend to do this right.

I gotta be honest with you – I am not the absolute best salesman on the planet every day. Some days I make good decisions about my business and others not so much. On this day, I had my best day ever as far as saying the right things and making the right decisions.

I asked him," What is the worst thing that could happen on this campus?" Now, I did have some idea what direction I wanted to go, but it would depend on how he answered this question. This could go from "Have a nice day" to my brain wanting to explode at this potential new opportunity.

His answer was, "a shooter".

I asked him," What would it look like?"

He said, "Chaos".

I said, "What would you like it to look like?"

He says, "I would like to have a command center where I

could view everything around the campus, figure out where the shooter was, and make decisions about what to do to eliminate the threat".

I said to him, " What if I told you that I could do that for you?"

He responded, "How soon could we get started?"

I said, "How about this afternoon?"

He told me that would be great. I then asked him who else at the campus would need to be involved. He mentioned that the VP and possibly the university president would need to be involved. He agreed to get me a few minutes with their group that afternoon to make sure they were willing and had the money to make this happen.

Now remember, I was pretty new with this company. I had been assigned a mentor who was twenty years younger than me, an OK sales rep, but she did have very good product knowledge. I called the office and asked to speak with her. They told me that she was in a meeting with the boss. I asked them to put me through to his office. I explained to them that I needed help and now. I had no idea how are products and systems worked, but I knew we had a really big fish on the line that could break free at any moment if we didn't act immediately. The boss told me that we had tried to work with this prospect before and never got anywhere. I asked him if he worked with the Chief, VP, and Pres. of the university. He said that no, we had never worked with them. I told him that I had a meeting with them that afternoon and needed someone to go with me that had been with the company for more than six months.

He canceled the rest of his meeting with my mentor and told her to go out that morning and figure out what was going on. When she got there, I took her around to meet the Chief and President's assistant. At that point she realized that what I had was real. I told her the scope of what I wanted to do – sell cameras, card access, and a campus monitoring system that along with a maintenance agreement would be close to $500,000. Our office, in fact our company, had never really done a project of that size before. They were also pessimistic about our chances this time as well. We went to the meeting that afternoon, and I shared my vision for their campus. I now had a monster prospect.

This was not my first or my last monster prospect. I am not sure how many I missed over the years and don't realize it, but as I said before, on this day and this prospect, it worked the way it should have in a perfect sales world. I was now working with Shaw University.

KEY POINT: YOU HAVE TO BE PREPARED TO TURN THE NUISANCE BUY INTO THE MONSTER ACCOUNT.

Chapter 5 – Execution

At Shaw University, I now had a prospect. I had a sponsor who really wanted the project to work, and quickly. He seemed like a guy I could work with – our personalities seemed to mesh. I had a decision maker that had the power to make this happen, and he was also on board. The president of the university was not interested in the details, but she wanted to feel and be safe on the campus. I had products and services to give them the security they desired. Now, I have to leave for two weeks for training.

Corporate sales training consists of learning how to sell ideas to the company's trainers. I have never seen a sales trainer that really understood how to effectively sell. Learn your products and services, and then find a mentor at your office who can teach you how to sell.

I was not very happy about having to leave my prospect for two weeks. What if they changed their mind or my office screwed it up. Both were very possible. I asked my mentor to conduct basic product surveys while I was gone but not to have any meetings with anyone other than our sponsor. I wanted the project to move, but I did not want the next steps done wrong. If each step is not done exactly right, you will not get the deal.

Executing the prospecting plan is crucial. If not done correctly, you can miss major opportunities or end up with a prospect list that is garbage, full of people that will never buy anything from you.

Ok, so how do we execute the perfect prospecting plan? Well, first you have to have a healthy mix in your plan. Ideally, you would have four appointments set each day with prospects in various stages of your pipeline, which we will talk about later. If not, you want to fill these times in meetings with suspects. These meetings should be with the highest level person in the organization that is involved with making decisions regarding your product line. It is easy to move down the ladder, difficult and sometimes impossible to move up the ladder. Do not fool yourself into thinking that it will work this time.

KEY POINT: YOU HAVE TO MEET WITH THE RIGHT PERSON IN THE LADDER OR YOU WILL NOT GET THIS CUSTOMER.

Very seldom will you be able to move up the ladder once you get started. The very fact that your sponsor did not include these individuals in your initial meeting indicates that they will not be there when you are trying to close the deal. Now you are relying on your sponsor to sell your project to their superiors. If they were that good at selling, they would be in sales. It's not going to happen. Never. Ever. Do not mislead yourself. Move on or get these people on board immediately. This is the first point in the process where you have to be right. I cannot express this enough. If you are not working with the right person, you would be better off taking a vacation than putting a false prospect into your pipeline. I have seen countless reps lose their job because they had full pipelines that never closed. Be honest with yourself.

Another key to your success is to maximize your territory. As my first boss once told me, you don't want to be a star salesman. This didn't make any sense to me. So he drew a star on the board and told me, "You want to drive to one area and work there all day. Plan your week so that you are covering a specific area each day instead of driving from here to there and then across the territory and spend four of your eight hours driving every day. He also said there are no customers in the office or in your car. You need to maximize the time each day that you are in front of buyers.

Part of maximizing your territory includes determining what areas are most apt to have the type of prospects you are targeting, such as urban, rural, etc. Urban areas obviously have more potential customers, but they also have more competition. When I first went into outside sales with Honeywell, I had a territory that encompassed four counties. One county included Canton, OH, which at that time was a vibrant city. It also had vibrant competitors. I was concerned that as a new rep, I was going to have to compete with seasoned, high quality reps from other companies.

Being the new rep, I am given the worst territory. I also have

Carroll County, which has four businesses in the whole county. They have a factory that builds aircraft tires, a company that builds some kind of industrial parts, a golf resort, and a bowling alley. My boss tells me not to go there, because it is the farthest area from our office and yields no business. He tells me to spend my time in Canton, which is in my territory and is much larger.

> Listing to this advice got the last two reps in this territory fired.

When I was working at my desk the first couple of weeks, the guy who was sitting next to me told me that the last two guys that had sat in that chair had been fired. I told him that meant it was time for a change, and that I was going to be there for awhile.

Carroll County was beautiful in the summer, and I did not want to go there during bad weather beginning in late fall, as it was about one hour away. Now typically I would say to work in your closest area, but I had an idea. I was guessing that if my company did not go to Carroll County, maybe others did not either.

I called and talked to the chief financial people at each of the businesses and set appointments with each of them. The first appointment was with the industrial prospect. Now, what we were selling was primarily preventive maintenance for HVAC equipment, and every business had multiple reps knocking on their door to sell these maintenance agreements.

When I went to the appointment, we were talking about maintenance, and I asked the prospect why they did not have a maintenance agreement in effect. The prospect told me that nobody had ever told them they needed one. I told them that I was there to tell them that they did need one. I got the contract.

I called the bowling alley and could not get an appointment with them. I also asked around and found out that bowling alleys typically did not do business with us, so after a few tries, I stopped calling them. This was early in my career, before I learned the power of cold calling.

Next, I called and set an appointment with the golf resort. They had their own water supply as well as cooled their facility with expensive electrical cooling systems that did not work well. They had an indoor swimming pool and an attached hotel.

The manager told me that he loved the idea of a preventive maintenance agreement, but that their equipment did not work well, so he wanted to fix it first. This was not an area I knew much about (or was really supposed to be selling), so I started to ask around the office. There were two sales reps that could ascertain what needed to be done and how to price it, but frankly, they were too busy to drive an hour to look at the new rep's problem account. Fortunately, I found out that one of our technicians lived an hour past this customer and rented an apartment in Akron near our office during the week so that he did not have to drive two hours each way from home.

I talked with him about meeting me on a Monday morning on his way into the office. This allowed him to spend Sunday night with his family. He thought that sounded like a great idea. I met him at the prospect's site and introduced him to my contact. My contact, who was both sponsor and decision maker, was impressed at our commitment to try and fix these long running problems. The technician liked the fact that a sales rep was bringing him in as an expert to trouble shoot the prospect's system. I learned that day that the technician could help me get business, especially in an arena that I did not know very well.

KEY POINT: OPERATIONS EMPLOYEES CAN HELP YOU SELL. A LOT.

I watched as the technician went through the system. I listened to what he told me was needed. He told me that this would allow him to stay home instead of in an apartment throughout the week if we could convert this prospect into a customer. As a result, he helped me put together proposals to repair and restore all of their equipment to a working condition as well as propose upgrades such as using lake water to cool their lodge and hotel. In the end, this was a great customer for Honeywell and me throughout my career selling for them. I also made friends with a number of the technicians who also helped me land customers once they found out that I respected what they could do and appreciated their help.

Each time I closed a customer in Carroll County, they now became my reference for other accounts in the area. In rural areas, references are very powerful in helping you close business. This helped us get into the tire manufacturer. We began by fixing their current equipment and then adding a maintenance contract.

As a new rep, I had just brought in three new accounts in an area with no competition. This helped me blow out my quota the first two years as well as learn what my company could do for prospects, as well as begin a list of powerful references, especially the golf resort. What prospect doesn't want to spend the afternoon having lunch, seeing how an innovative system works, and then play golf in the afternoon? What a great reference. Also, the tire manufacturer? A subsidiary of Goodyear Tire & Rubber Co. Here I was the new guy, and I had the two best references in the office, not to mention third highest sales out of six reps my first year.

KEY POINT: LOOK FOR THE PROSPECTS NOBODY ELSE WANTS – IF YOU CAN CONVERT THEM, THEY WILL BE LOYAL TO YOU.

It may seem like I had a lot of luck early on. Luck in sales is a direct result of developing a smart plan and working hard. Good things will happen for you. I can't really explain it, but it works.

Developing a mix of prospecting techniques is key to your success. I cannot tell you what will work best for you – you just have to keep trying all of them until you get a feel for what works best.

Not being a star salesman helps you incorporate and maximize your prospecting efforts. I really tried to have four set appointments each day, typically at 9:30, 11:00, 1:30, and 3:00. This gave me a half hour in the morning and a half hour at the end of the day for anything I might need at the office or for conference calls, etc. Here is where flexibility becomes important. Prospects or customers will cancel or reschedule appointments. What do you do if you are an hour away from the office and you have a cancellation? You cold call. Just start driving around the area you are in looking for prospects that you may not have seen through your normal suspect investigations using Google, etc. Sometimes you just see something that looks right. Now, I agree that this is not the most productive use of your time. I would rather be closing a deal than cold calling, however, sometimes you just have some extra time on your hands. If you did not uncover a gem online, maybe your competition has not either.

I was working with my mentor rep at ADT one day, and we had some time to kill. Our client at Shaw University was terrible about setting appointments, so believe it or not, many of our meetings with him were held by waiting outside his office before or after lunch, hoping to catch him in his walk through the parking lot. I know, sales experts will tell you that if you cannot get an appointment, what are the odds this guy is going to buy from you? I agree, however, this $500,000 account did business this way. It kept out the competition.

As a result, we had to set aside a lot of time on a day we wanted to meet with him. I don't remember the specifics of that day, but we seemed to have the entire afternoon free after we met with him for two minutes in the parking lot. Those meetings were important though, because others in their organization did most of the work with us; we just wanted his ok for each step along the way. I have had other customers that worked that way as well. I had one school superintendent who never was involved, but on the day of the contract signing, he walked in, signed the contract, and walked back out.

So with this extra time on our hands, we decided to cold call up and down the street in downtown Raleigh. My co-worker hated cold calling, and I still had limited knowledge as to what our company's capabilities were. So the plan was that I would walk in and introduce myself, and if they were interested, she would talk about services and solutions. We did this for a couple of hours with no real interest, except one. We ran across an old ADT customer that wanted to upgrade their business security in a number of ways. This turned into a nice upgrade and maintenance account as well as a project at another facility that they owned. This was definitely worth a day of walking around being told no thirty or forty times.

We still had some time left that day and were talking about a new development that we had tried to get into, and after a year, we had made no progress. We were trying to work with the general contractors who kept giving us excuses, but no business. This was not our typical customer. It was a local housing authority with large residential neighborhoods. We decided that we would stop into their headquarters a few blocks away.

We walked in, told the receptionist who we were, and started talking about the project we were interested in. We told her who we were working with, and asked who we should be talking to at the headquarters. She directed us to a person who met with us and told us who was spearheading this project. It was a team of two guys, and she passed on our info to them. We called and set a meeting with these guys. It turns out that the individuals running that project were not really interested in what modern commercial security could do for them. These guys believed, after our conversation that they should be looking into new technology such as that offered by our company instead of what was being proposed.

We found out later that these guys were in IT and had to work with the outdated technology being specified and installed into their projects. They went to the executive director of the agency and convinced him to take a look into the options.

At this point, they were our sponsors, and our competition was actually another department within the organization. This would obviously change our approach, because although I have had detractors within companies before, it was not the entire engineering and construction department. We will talk more about this and the other accounts more as we go through the chapters, but for now, just know that this cold call turned into over $600,000 in business over the next two to three years.

KEY POINT: COLD CALLING AND OTHER METHODS OF PROSPECTING THAT TURN INTO CONVERSATIONS WITH POTENTIAL CUSTOMERS ARE VITAL TO YOUR EVERYDAY ACTIVITIES. THEY ARE YOUR FUTURE.

Section 2: Relationships

Chapter 6 – Establishing a Basic Relationship

Establishing a relationship with your prospect is important. Most people buy from people that they like. It is probably not required, but it is close to required. Hopefully, you have a good working relationship with your sponsor. It helps provide honesty and the ability to persuade your prospect into becoming your customer.

I can honestly say that I have liked most of my customers. There have been a couple of detractors that were not my best friend, but other than that, your prospect needs to like you and you like them. There have been two instances that I can think of where I really did not like my sponsor, and I am sure that it affected our relationship. I don't think they really liked me either.

The first instance of dislike came when we had a long-term contract, and my sponsor retired. He was one of my favorite customers, but the guy who reported to him and later became my primary contact did not really want us there. He had a strong relationship with the former supplier, and I don't think he really ever gave our organization a chance. We had a long-term contract, and we honored it to the letter and did a great job for this customer, but once my sponsor retired, we kept the contracts we had but never got any new ones.

This can happen when you have long-term accounts. Sometimes, the person you are working with changes for a variety of reasons. You can try to convert this person or just keep it very businesslike, never make any mistakes, and hope for the best.

One of the things that will happen to you once you are a superstar sales rep is that you will be given large accounts that management thinks are being mismanaged or the rep handling the account quits, gets fired, or gets promoted. This has happened to me on two occasions, both involving not only my office's largest client, but the largest in the company.

On the first occasion, I found out that my sponsor liked to eat. So do I. He liked to eat huge Italian lunches and drink four vodka tonics with lunch. Once a week I drove an hour, took him to lunch, bought him a $50 lunch and talked with him about the business we were doing. I did over $4 million in business with this account during my last year there. It was worth my time and money. When your quota is less than $500,000, and someone is willing to spend eight times that every year, it is worth buying him lunch every day if you have to.

On the second occasion, I was assigned a $400,000 account that the boss and field technician for this customer thought was being mismanaged. I disagreed with their assessment and told them so. I took the account knowing that the technician, sales manager, regional manager, and "sponsor" were all ahead of me in leading this account, but I took it anyway.

It was very difficult to manage and lead this account as my thoughts and ideas were not really welcomed. There existed a strong set of relationships that did not include the previous rep. I thought I could work my magic and become the lead on the account. Wasn't going to happen. The sponsor was not a sponsor for me. I reached out to the decision maker, who seemed like I could work with, but as our relationship started to grow, he retired. I had no direct line to the new decision makers, and the sponsor told me that he would rather work through the technicians and that I did not need to meet with him. The sales manager somehow thought he had some rapport with the sponsor, but he probably had less than me. The regional manager sometimes visited the sponsor without my knowledge, so as you have probably figured out already, I had no relationship at all with this customer.

I basically decided to let the system work as it was. The only thing that I did was provide the sponsor with technical data on new products as they came out. I also knew that I was going to get whatever business they decided to give me, so I did not discount any products or services. I did convince them to add maintenance services at a much higher level than before and immediately upon purchase. That was all I could accomplish with no good working relationship. The only good part is that through working internally and externally with this customer, I increased their business from $400,000 to $1,500,000 within two years. At that point, this customer was significantly impacting my ability to work with any other customers in a positive manner, so after two years, I asked to be taken off of the account.

There are people that you can work with well, and due to their or your personality, there are people that just don't mesh with your style. It's not really anyone's fault, just recognize when it happens and move on. On a long-term basis, you will be farther ahead.

Once you have had some success, you will have a good idea as to what your ideal sponsor looks like. I can tell you mine. Male, 55 years old, could use to lose 20 pounds, is pretty laid back, but knows what he wants and expects you to get him there. It doesn't matter whether I was 25 years old or whether it was last year, almost every one of my best customers fits into this category. I can't tell you why, but I can tell you that it is real.

How do we establish a basic working relationship? Initially, it has to be based on the prospect believing that there may be a chance that you may have something he wants. This has to be done on a low key basis. I have tried to shock a couple of prospects into making a decision or working with me toward a solution with a grim prediction as to what was going to happen if they did not do something. It never worked.

What works is finding out a basic idea or two as to whether their business may be in the market for what you have. This is done very conversationally without promises or boasts about your company. You may want to tell the prospect that you have no idea whether or not you can do anything for them, but based on the type of business they have, you have had quite a bit of success helping customers just like them. At that point, just ask them some easy questions and give them a glimpse of how you have helped others. Be careful at this point about overselling, they may ask you to prove it down the road.

You may ask what kind of business they are in or what issues they are facing. Just easy questions to get some idea as to whether they may have the desire, ability, and authority to buy anything from you. Ask them for some information – do they provide it willingly, not at all, or promise to send it to you later? This first meeting should give you an idea as to what it will be like to work with them throughout the selling process. Make sure that you ask enough questions to get them thinking as to the benefits of working with you. I once had a prospect that really needed our help, but he told me that he did not want any work being done in the summer because he wanted to spend his summer traveling to baseball games and did not want any projects to get in the way. I told him, "Thanks for the meeting", and got out of there as quickly as possible.

I guess I could have taken him to a baseball game, but it was obvious that he had no real interest in getting any work done. I have also found little value to wining and dining prospects. I enjoy taking customers to lunch or golf or any activity that provides them some fun and builds our relationship, but I can honestly say that I have never gotten new business from the golf course. I will take a prospect to lunch if we are visiting a customer site for referral or something like that. A reasonable lunch will help to build the relationship and allow the prospect to discuss what they saw during the visit while we plan the next steps in the cycle. I do not want the prospect to think that I am buying them lunch to try and get their business. A small lunch after a site visit at a reasonable price builds not only the relationship but also integrity and professionalism (Make sure you order something that you are not going to eat with your fingers or get all over your shirt – it ruins the whole reason you were buying them lunch). Also, don't drink alcohol at the lunch. You want to build this as a long-term relationship very carefully. Remember why you are here – to get some serious business from this prospect.

Don't spend too much time during this stage. You are not here to sell or promise anything. You are just trying to figure out if this organization has the money and ability to buy what you sell. You want to figure out if you have anything they need. Do you think this person can serve as a sponsor to move this through the organization, or even better, is this person the decision maker that you feel will buy from you?

The more time you spend past 30-45 minutes is typically not well spent. Answer any professional or personal questions asked of you, size this person up, and schedule a follow-up meeting. Tell him/her you will email some info, and let them know what info you need from them.

This is the beginning of the give and take that is necessary to have a healthy working relationship as well as get your sponsor invested in the project.

KEY POINT: The object of this stage is solely to get the prospect interested in looking into what you may have to offer them. Revealing too much or promising too much can lead to problems down the road.

Chapter 7 – Building Trust

Once your suspect becomes a prospect, you need to start building trust. I used to tell my manager who was always asking how soon we could bring in a specific account, "You don't ask someone for $500,000 on the first visit". You need to build trust in order to maximize your first and subsequent orders. The more the prospect trusts you and your organization, the more they will be willing to invest in the project.

Building trust takes some time, usually a direct correlation to the size of the project. Trust is also correlated to the business climate. Some parts of the country require business and personal trust. Others take the lowest or best bid and rely on their attorneys for any problems. Regardless, a bond of trust between your customer and you can make your life easier and more profitable.

Just like every aspect of extreme selling, there is a specific formula for building trust:

1. Be honest. If you don't know the answer, just tell them that you don't know but will find out. Humility builds trust. If the installation is not going well, admit it, and work out a realistic project schedule. Remember, you want more business and will only get more if the customer is satisfied with what I like to call Phase I. I like to make sure that everyone, my company and my customer, know that we are creating a long-term relationship. Call your customer with any bad news. You want them to hear it from you and in a way that includes some options for resolution rather than someone telling them they have a big problem.
2. Prove what you are saying. Don't tell your prospect how great you are, offer to show them. Offer to take them to your best customer so that a neutral third party can tell them how great you and your company are. If possible, take them somewhere fun as well. We had a major sports arena as a client. Who doesn't want to see the inner workings of a pro sports franchise, especially if they are rehearsing for an event or changing out the

floor from basketball to hockey. Take them a couple of places if you can. Customers love to brag about their great decisions and systems. You build a ton of trust just by letting your prospects talk to your best customers. It reinforces the great decision that your customer made, making them want to buy more from you, so this is a double-win. I have used site visits for almost every large client. If this is a super large potential customer, take them to your factory for a tour or somewhere impressive and fun that involves travel. All of this also helps get your customer committed to the project. Your competitors probably will not do any of this, so you should be starting to pull ahead of the competition.
3. Trust happens outside of the prospect's office. Have your customer go through a site survey of their equipment with you. Ask them questions. Let them see the detail which you incorporate into your site surveys. Let them meet your management team during one of these surveys. Managers do much better in this arena then during proposals, as they do

not always have the same agenda for the meeting. All of these meetings help build rapport. Throw in a lunch or two. Even if you cannot buy them lunch do to corporate policies, sharing a meal with someone builds the relationship.
4. If your proposal will include technical information, bring your supplier along if you can trust them and they are good with people. They will be able to address the IT department or engineering questions better than you, and it shows that you utilize a team to deliver customer satisfaction to your customers, not just you. If someone is spending $500,000, they expect to see a team. Just make sure you talk to your team each time they will interact so that they do not sidetrack your plan with their own ideas. If your plan gets off track, you could lose the project.
5. If you have a common hobby or sports team with your prospect, it is good to have light discussion about them. I would not let it become too forced, or it appears disingenuous.

6. The bigger the project, the more trust you will need. As each visit builds a little more trust, large projects need a lot of face time to build the level of trust that you need to close the deal. Also, every time you meet with your customer, you are providing more opportunity for the prospect to tell you something else they would like to have, especially during site surveys.
7. Start looking for supporters, detractors, other sponsors, or decision-makers during this stage. The sooner you recognize who they are and which role they may play, the earlier you can involve them in the project at the right points. For instance, inviting a detractor who works in operations to meet with your engineer or go on a site visit may convert him/her into a sponsor or at least neutralize them. You probably want to invite decision makers to any major referral visits – again they are fun and show your best side. This also gives you an opportunity to build trust with these other individuals as well as find out what their priorities are – you may want to throw something into the project that will

help move them to your side in any negotiations.
8. If you are having difficulty building a relationship with one or more of the individuals within your prospect organization, think about bringing someone else onto your team that can provide what that prospect team member needs in order to support your goals. On almost every major project that I have closed, I have brought in one or more managers, sales reps, engineers, or operations technicians to work with one of the prospects that does not seem satisfied with the answers I give them. Maybe we just don't hit it off, or maybe they are looking for some level of detail or explanation that I am not providing. You cannot be all things to all people, but you may know who can add to the team to keep the project moving along on the right path.
9. What you are trying to convey at this stage is not that everything will work out perfectly, but that they can trust you to take care of their interests, and if something does go wrong, they can call you and you will help them find a way to fix it.

KEY POINT: THE MORE THE PROSPECT TRUSTS YOU AND YOUR ORGANIZATION, THE MORE THEY WILL BUY.

Chapter 8 – Creating Needs and Wants

At this point in the process, you are not selling anything to the prospect. You have built some basic rapport and trust, giving you an idea that this prospect will probably work with you and become a customer if you are able to provide some solutions to problems, concerns, or issues that they may have. Throughout the initial rapport and trust building phases, you probably have started to get an idea as to how you may be able to help this customer with some of their needs.

Now is the time where you start to formalize these needs into something that you can work with. This is primarily done through asking questions and verifying your abilities to address their issues.

Obviously, you know your products and services, both features and benefits, so you want to lead the discussion in the areas in which you excel. You want to ask as many open-ended questions as possible in an effort to uncover your prospect's most pressing needs. It is vital that you uncover needs that would be on your prospect's top ten most wanted list and preferably their top five list. The closer to the top of the list that each need is, the more likely that your prospect is going to be motivated to enact these changes.

If the needs that you uncover are not pressing needs for your customer, they are more likely not to purchase goods and services from you. Most prospects are focused on their immediate needs, just as is any individual in their personal life. They also have numerous other parties vying for their spending dollars every day. As they only have a limited amount of time and money, most prospects will spend their time and money in an effort to address their most pressing concerns.

So how does the top rep get onto the top five needs list of the prospect? They listen to the answers of their prospect to the open ended questions in a manner where they are constantly thinking whether they have any products, services, or a combination which will land them on the top five list. The top rep is creative in his/her approach.

Here is an example of how this worked for me. I received a call that a local university needed a panic button as one of their leadership team members was concerned about personal safety. There may have been threats against this person. I found out that I needed to work with the VP of Facilities.

After a number of phone calls that yielded disorganized results in the area of setting an appointment with the VP, finally told him that I would stop over the next morning, and we would try and find a time to meet. Of course, when I got there, he was busy out somewhere on the campus. I met with his administrative assistant who obviously had no purchasing power or the ability to walk me through the process.

Eventually, the VP made it back to his office and very aggressively let me know that he had no time for me and just wanted to buy one panic button. Keep in mind that he called me, not the other way around. This let me know that he would be difficult to deal with. He does not set meeting times and was disrespectful when I arrived. At this point, all I knew was that he wanted to make a $50 purchase that I would probably regret at some point. In addition, I had no idea what we would tie this panic button into that would enable us to alarm the police, so I could probably either sell him a button that would never really work right or a basic system that would cost at least $3,000 for a button that may never be used. This did not feel like a good deal for anyone. So what do I do now?

I wanted to do business with this university because they would qualify on everyone's list as a strategic account. They were large, had lots of money, lots of needs, and everyone in the area knew who they were. All I had to do was find a more effective sponsor that would help be do business with them without alienating the VP. I asked him who else might be involved in the decision to install a panic button. He told me that their campus police chief would want to talk with me about the button. I told him that would be fine, and he pointed to the Campus Police office, glad to be rid of me.

When I arrived, I asked to see the Chief of Police, as I had been directed. He invited me into his office and asked me to sit down across from his desk. I did so, and he told me that he was aware of the situation and was willing to help out in any way that he could. I shared with him my meeting with the VP and asked him if they currently had any type of security system for the campus. He told me that they did not, but that he wished they did. He also told me that they used to have some cameras, but those had all been destroyed.

What followed was the best questioning I ever did in my entire sales career. I simply asked him, "What is the worst case scenario for you as Chief of Police?" You notice that this is an open-ended question. I had no idea where he may go with this question, but at this point, I had no sale and little hope for one. He answered me with one word and one word only. Shooter. That's all he said. Shooter. I asked him, " What does that look like?" He answered again with one word. Chaos. That's right, shooter and chaos. Now what should I do? What would you do? Think about it before you read the next paragraph. What would you say or do in response to those answers?

I said to him, "What would you like it to look like?" You were expecting something profound, weren't you? You spent money to buy this book, and this is all you get??? That's right, because it is about asking the right open-ended questions to get the answers that you need to determine if you can sell your products and services to the prospect. Had he answered with, "I don't know", I would have needed to probe further to try to get to his needs.

Why am I spending so much time with this guy anyway? Well, he has a position of buying and influencing power. He is receptive to my questioning. He seems like a nice guy who cares about doing the best thing for his employer. I like him. Now why does it matter if I like him or not. Well, I suppose it doesn't, but it is more difficult to build a trusting, business relationship if you don't like your prospect or he/she doesn't like you.

So how did he answer this last question? Here is what he said to me. "I would have a command center where I could go with university officials and local police. We would be able to look at cameras that would show us where the shooter was and where he was going. I would like to be able to shut down areas so that he could not get in other buildings, and if we had all of that, we could make better decisions as to how to proceed".

As a sales rep who sold command center hardware and software, cameras, and swipe card systems to track and disallow entry into buildings, as well as video analytics, this was the best answer I ever heard. This prospect wanted to buy everything that I sold and lots of it. So now what do I say to him in response? I said, "I can provide all of that for you." He replied that he would like that, but it would have to be in phases due to their financial situation. WOW! Not only does he want to buy all of my stuff, but he wants to buy from me every quarter or every year until this entire campus in locked down and monitored. The only thing better than a customer is a repeat customer.

I called the office and told them that I needed some help. We made arrangements to start doing a needs analysis the following Monday. I will be the first to tell you that I was never the most technologically knowledgeable person on the sales team. I didn't need to be. We had technicians and managers at the office that were there to work with me to help put together the pieces and parts to help meet the needs of the customer.

KEY POINT: CREATING NEEDS AND WANTS IS ABOUT ASKING THE RIGHT OPEN-ENDED QUESTIONS TO FIND OUT WHAT YOUR CUSTOMER REALLY WANTS AND IS WILLING TO PAY FOR.

Chapter 9 – ProjectTeam

Assembling your project team is vital to securing the business. Your potential buyer has many different needs, wants, and dislikes. This comes out through the various individuals that comprise the team at your prospect's location. The first thing is to figure out who is on the team or influences the team for this purchase. What I am talking about is anyone who is going to have a say into what is purchased, if anything, how much, and how often.

The first thing that you have to do is determine who the decision makers and influencers are as well as the strength of each person in the decision-making process. Those individuals that may be on the prospect's team who do not care about the outcome or are not really consulted do not really matter in assembling your team, but you have to ensure that you are accurately portraying each influencing individual. If you get this wrong, you probably do not get the deal.

These individuals and their preferences will determine what and how you present to this customer. This means that you have to get it right because if you miss a need or want, or over or under estimate the strength of that individual, your team may not be assembled in a way that maximizes your opportunities for success with this prospect.

So, what does this look like in real life? Well, first you have your sponsor. This is the person that you are relying on to move this project through their system to a signed agreement at the end, as well as future projects. The fact that you are this far with this prospect says to me that you have built a trust relationship with this person, and you strongly believe that this person can make it happen. As such, this person is probably your responsibility unless they also have specific needs that you personally cannot address, in which case we will add someone to meet their additional needs.

OK, so we have started with you and the prospect. The next step is to determine who can influence your prospect. Is there a decision-maker or influencer that is going to have a big impact on whether or not this sale happens? This individual may need someone on the project team that is there specifically to build trust and a working relationship that will ensure that we have two strong sponsors or decision-makers on our side. If they are sponsors, it definitely strengthens the possibility that we will get this deal when there are two people pitching our idea to the organization and decision-makers as opposed to just one.

In many cases, this second individual is complementary to our sponsor in that they come from a different area of the business. This is why it can be vital that we have someone on the team that can build a different type of relationship with this second person, as their needs are typically different. In my case, this typically meant a more technical person than me. My prospect is usually most interested in the big picture type of solution, as I attract sponsors that lean that direction as that is how I approach an organization. I try to create a picture of what their organization will look like with my products and services. As a result, my contact person is not usually super technical. The second person on their team typically is technical. I cannot address both of their needs at the same time. That is not my focus. My focus is on the big picture solution. This can frustrate the second team member as they have numerous questions about the technical aspects of the project, such as IT components, how does my equipment work, how will it tie in with their existing infrastructure, etc.

As a result, I usually add a second team member in the area of engineering or product knowledge to work with this person. I usually add this person before I build my team, as I want a second opinion of the opportunity that we may have and the difficulties that we may face. Though I typically go with my gut feelings about whether this prospect can be converted, it is nice to have a knowledgeable second opinion. In addition, I get the opportunity to stop talking and watch my prospect and other team member as they respond to my technical person. This is something that is not easy to do when you are engaged in conversation with your prospect.

It should be somewhat obvious, but this is typically your most important team member. They are the first person from your company that you are introducing to your prospect. As a result, your prospect looks at this person to get an idea how your company works. It is an interesting dynamic because they do not look at this person as a salesperson. This brings an additional layer of credibility to the project, as they assume this person has nothing at stake and will not try to sell them on anything. This typically causes them to relax a little and put their trust in your partner.

This team member needs to be a combination of technical ability and sales savvy. They are helping to fill a niche with your customer, but they are also primary in helping you sell this deal, as the person that they are responsible for may be the key to getting this deal done. Your prospect already likes the idea somewhat, or you would not be this far with their company. Now comes in a second person that provides needed technical expertise while supporting your sales process.

This second person on your team may be all that you need to separate you from everyone else that has walked through their door. They now are working with a "team" from your company, and it appears that one of your team members is actually on their side, helping to educate them so that they can make the best decision for them.

Depending on the size and scope of the project, you may need to add a third person to your team. This may be based on the size of their team. If they have five people on the team making this decision, you may need more than two people to meet their discovery needs, as it can be difficult to build relationships with five diverse individuals when there are only two of you.

The decision to add this individual is probably not as vital as the first person you added, but you still need to add the right person. You have to decide if you need an operational person, such as the Installation or Service Manager, or do you need to add your Sales Manager or Branch/Regional Manager.

Your decision rests on a couple of different areas. The first is whether there are still any gaps in coverage of the needs of your prospect's team. Is there a specific area that is not being addressed? That should be your first thought as you continue to build your team. In addition, IT has now become a major player in any business decision. In the past, I would typically err on the side of bringing in the sales manager. This person understands that we are there to make a sale and should act accordingly. This is another set of ears and eyes to make sure that we are covering all of our prospect's needs. In addition, this person is typically able to get us additional resources at a higher level, such as a customer visit to one of our other sites or a visit to our manufacturing facility.

The downside to adding an operational person to your team is that they typically are not sales oriented. As a result, it is not uncommon that they will start leading the conversation into areas that you would not like discussed at this point in the process. Because they are an operational manager, they have credibility, again not a sales person so they will tell the truth. And yes, they will tell the truth, including things like, "Just so you know, we are really backed up right now. I hope you don't need this completed in the next six months, because we are on this really big job, and we are having hardware and software programs, probably a bad batch from the factory, as well as being shorthanded, so I don't see any way we would be able to get to this for quite a while". Now, what they said may be true in their mind, but that may not be an accurate portrayal for the customer. They may not be aware that extra technicians are being hired, or this job is different from the other one, or any number of factors, however, that statement which I have heard on more than one occasion can suck all of the air out of the room and your project in one statement, destroying everything you have been working on for three months.

However, there has been a major change in team selling. Within the past few years, prospects have added an IT person to the team to ensure that the project can be supported by the IT team as well as the IT infrastructure of the prospect's system. This makes it almost inevitable that you are going to have bring in operational support to your team.

The best way that I have found to do this is to wait until IT shows up. They are typically not brought into the prospect's team until they are getting serious about committing to the project. This is a good sign for you as it strengthens the possibility that this project is going to happen. Once IT shows up, I like to schedule a separate meeting for my ops person to meet with IT and ensure them that the systems will be compatible. I also brief our IT person before the meeting and let them know that if any deal breakers or serious problems in compatibility arise during their discussions, just let me know what hardware or software is needed, and I will make sure that it is included in the project.

This seems to pacify their IT staff and our operations team. This meeting is typically held separate from our sponsor(s), so the damage is minimal if our operations manager makes statements that could kill the project. Most IT managers know that there is significant lead time as well as delays throughout installation, as these issues are where they spend their days. They do not get upset at these statements, as they almost expect that to be the case.

There is one way to minimize any potential damage from including an operations or sales manager. Start including them in your team strategy meetings for this prospect as soon as you realize this could be a big project. If they feel that they are part of the process, they are less apt to get out to the prospect's location and say whatever might pop up in their head.

There may be other team members that you need to maximize your chances of landing this prospect. There may be other sponsors or decision makers that you feel need a certain type of person to move them over to your side. This could be a C-suite individual who only wants to talk to other executives. That's ok, let the two of them go somewhere for a power lunch to make this person feel special. It could be someone who is not a sponsor, decision maker, or influencer. It could just be a "no" person. Their job is not to help things get done, it is just to try to kill anything that comes along. I had a prospect tell me one time that the project looked really good, but he did not want to spend his summer dealing with this, because he wanted to take off a lot of time to go watch the Cincinnati Reds play baseball. Unfortunately, this person was absolutely necessary to make this deal happen, so we walked away and decided to go back if he ever retired.

KEY POINT: YOUR TEAM NEEDS TO FULFILL ALL OF THE NEEDS AND WANTS OF YOUR PROSPECT'S TEAM. BEFORE YOU MOVE TO THE NEXT STAGE, IT IS VITAL THAT YOUR TEAM MATCHES THEIR TEAM.

Chapter 10 – Matching Services with Needs/Wants

Matching the services you decide to offer with the needs and wants of your prospect should not be difficult if you have done everything that needs to be done up to this point. You are going to find out very soon if you have done everything necessary.

Let's review for a minute or two. Did you build a solid foundation with your sponsor? That should have included question and answer periods that would provide you with an accurate list of both needs and wants. Did you identify everyone who is a stakeholder in this project? Did you build the right team to help you build trust with these individuals or groups so that you can be confident that you know their needs and wants? Do they have real needs and wants that you can address? No organization is going to spend significant money with you if they do not really need or want anything. Have you identified those individuals in the prospect organization that can say no to the project? Do you know what it will take to pacify them so that they will not say no?

Most importantly, did you shortchange any of the steps? I once gave a proposal for several hundred thousand dollars and knew that there was no way they were going to buy anything. How did I know this? Well, we had only known this prospect for less than thirty days. We had only met with this sponsor a couple of times, and frankly, he seemed too busy to deal with us each time we were there. Nobody gives you hundreds of thousands or millions of their company's money if you have not taken the time to get to get them to like you and earn their trust.

However, my sales manager was in a big rush to get this deal signed, so we went and proposed this huge proposal to this prospect. And what do you think happened? He responded with an OK, thanks for the proposal. He was not invested in this project, and if he was, I don't know that we would have been his first choice as the vendor. I knew we were not going to get the deal. In most cases, you do not get a second chance. You just get the response, "Thanks, we'll call you when we make a decision". They have already made their decision, and it is not you and not today.

Fortunately, this guy was not our true sponsor. I was able to undo the damage that my manager had inflicted and work with the new sponsor to gain multiple projects that were very large.

You cannot shortchange any of the steps. If you do, you will be wondering what happened. Even the prospect that tells you they need the proposal this week needs to be cultivated. If you rush the process, you will give a great proposal and never hear from that prospect again. Then you will wonder what happened. It's the customer's fault, your operations team's fault, your references' fault. No, it's your fault because you cut short some of your work.

KEY POINT: TAKE WHATEVER TIME IS NEEDED TO BUILD A VERY STRONG RELATIONSHIP WITH THE PROSPECT. DO NOT SKIP ANY OF THE STEPS.

I cannot stress this enough, as this is where deals fall apart, but sales reps do not realize it until their prospects tell them that they will call them later. They are not going to call – you did not do everything you needed to do to make this work. If you do not get the project, look back to this step to determine where you missed it. It is not the customer's job to make this sale happen for you. If you do not get the sale, it is on you.

So how do we match our needs and services to the customer's needs and wants? This is incredibly simple – give them what they want. Do not give them the hot item of the week, nobody really wants that, this is why your company is trying to basically give it away. It is expensive and solves few problems. It has a high profit margin, but provides little customer service of their needs and wants. Stop listening to what your company wants you to push.

KEY POINT: GIVE THE CUSTOMER WHAT THEY WANT.

How hard is that? Look in your bag of things to sell and see if any of them match what the prospect wants or needs. If there is nothing, why are you still talking to this prospect? You have to take their needs and wants and see if you have anything that will satisfy their list of needs. If you are at this step and do not have anything that meets their needs, then I am not sure what you have been doing. If the customer wants a new company truck and all you sell are motorcycles, you should have realized this and ran from this prospect very early on.

OK, so assuming that their need and want list are items that you can address with your products and services, then let's look at what we have to offer and put together a proposal that addresses all or most of the prospect's needs. Try to include goods and services. A prospect would rather receive an all in one proposal that addresses all of their needs and services, as well as ongoing maintenance, than a cheap quote that really does not solve all of their problems. Trust me, in competitive situations, I was always the highest cost, sometimes double my competition. Yet I typically won the business. Why? Because I matched their needs and wants with our products and services.

Sales organizations spend inordinate amounts of money on training new reps how to sell. Do role plays, take personality tests, etc. as needed to get the new rep ready. But their focus is on training the rep to find a way to force their products and services on prospects. Now I know that this sometimes does work, but it is not the best way, the right way, the professional way to provide your future customers with a strategic plan of buying from you the things that they and their organization want and need.

Instead, teach these new reps how to uncover needs and wants. Selling customers on the hot product or service of the day will land some deals, but overall long-term sales will pale in contrast to the repeat customer that can be generated through the process described in this book and especially this chapter.

It is not really that difficult. Spend time during sales training teaching new reps how to ask open-ended questions. Sales is not about talking, it is about listening. Teach reps how to ask questions that will put the prospect in the best position to provide answers that include needs and wants that the business will actually buy.

As mentioned earlier, I have seen some good reps sell prospects products and services that they do not need. This is not only possible, it is not really that hard. It just takes perseverance, which is one quality of most successful reps. Unfortunately, this does not build long-term trust with the customer, because they may eventually realize that they do not really need what they just bought. It may incrementally improve their business but probably not enough to do repeat projects or become great references for your future prospects.

Instead, spend time getting very good at figuring out what your customer really needs and wants. Questioning without promising or selling will get you to their true needs. If you are not uncovering something that your company offers that they need, you are either not getting to details for one reason or another, or maybe, they just do not need anything that you offer. There could be a variety of reasons for this, as they may already have state of the art products or services, or they do not need what you have.

This is not usually the case. Fortunately, technology makes everything obsolete very quickly, but how do you find out for sure what they need? Again, build some trust. Don't sell – listen! Just ask them about their business and what things cause them the most headaches. You may have to give them a brief view on what you offer to ensure that they are on the right path with their answers to your questions, but almost any realistic answers should lead you to something that you can use to try and see if your products and services meet their needs.

KEY POINT: ASK AND LISTEN, ASK AND LISTEN, SHOW INTEREST IN THEM AND THEIR BUSINESS. THIS IS NOT THE TIME TO SELL, THIS IS THE TIME TO SEE WHAT THEY NEED.

Chapter 11 – Trial Balloon

Every sales rep starts to get nervous when it is time to prepare the proposal for their prospect. Up until this point, they have a promising prospect on their list of prospects that they are working for. This keeps the sales manager happy, as you have a list of prospects that you are working with that are going to bring in revenue for your office and keep you employed as well as paid.

Unfortunately, you are getting really close to the point where you have to present your proposal to the prospect. This is also about the time that your manager starts asking you when you are going to close this deal. The stress level is about to go up dramatically as this prospect that meant nothing to the company is now the basis for payroll for next month as well as your job security.

I am no different than anyone else. I do not like the unknown when it comes to my job and income, and I do not want to be told no by the prospect I have been working with for a couple of months or more than a year.

There is a way to ensure that neither of these things happens. It is called a trial balloon. A trial balloon is when you test the prospect's desire to do business with you by giving them an idea of what the project is going to entail that you intend to propose.

This is probably the easiest part of the entire process. It also gives you valuable information so that when you make your proposal, you are sure that they are going to say yes.

Prior to submitting the trial balloon, this is also the perfect time to take your prospect on a site visit to your best customer to show them how great you and your company are. This may include just your sponsor, but ideally it would involve a group of the decision makers from your prospect company. If this is not feasible, I would at least give them a list of some great references to further solidify your relationship going into the proposal. It also gives you another opportunity to determine your prospect's commitment to working with you on this project. If they turn down the visit or do not call any of your references, that is a red flag that they are not committed to moving forward with you. Every prospect loves a site visit. It gets them out of the office for an afternoon and gives them an opportunity to sway any naysayers on their team.

This site visit should be a visible customer if possible. Take them to a sports arena or major hospital or college. In other words, take them somewhere impressive so that they can see you are more than capable of taking care of their account. Also, try to take them somewhere where your customer loves to talk about how great your company and you are. Customers love to brag about the great decisions they make.

At the end of the visit, let them know that prior to the proposal, you are going to send them a general idea of what you are proposing to make sure that it includes everything they want at the right price. This also gives them an opportunity to prepare their colleagues to support the proposal once it is time.

What you do is write up a basic general idea of what your proposal is going to be. It should include the following items:

1. The general scope of what you intend to propose, as in buildings included, general parts/pieces such as lighting, HVAC, windows, automation, etc. (This does not include any quantities or specific information).
2. General services being added to the ongoing maintenance of the project. This is important because it gives the customer a way of staying your customer once the initial installation is complete. It also lets your customer know that you do not intend to abandon him as soon as he signs the contract. He knows that you will be with him throughout the installation and ongoing performance of the system being installed.
3. Very general long-term plan showing how there will be an additional project each year going forward. You are letting him know that you are not trying to get all of their money upfront and run. You are going to be taking care of

his needs for approximately five years down the road.
4. **You do not include any pricing in this trial balloon. This is designed to make sure that you have the project components that your prospect wants without any items that they don't.**

This is not delivered in person. This is the one exception to maximizing face time with your prospect. This is designed to be very low key. It is like you are giving your customer unique insight into how your company works prior to the proposal. It also strengthens the bond that you have with your sponsor, because you are giving him a sneak preview that nobody else is getting. This should be dropped off, scanned and emailed, or some other casual way that puts no pressure on your prospect. Call him a day or so later to make sure that he received it, and ask him if he has had a chance to look it over. Once he has, ask him if this is what he is looking for. Ask him if he has had a chance to go over anything relevant with any of his team that will be involved with making the decision at the proposal.

None of this will appear in your sales training. Your sales manager will not understand why you are doing this. They will ask you why you don't just go deliver the proposal. The answer is because the one time that my manager pushed me into a proposal before I felt the prospect was ready, the proposal turned into chaos and they almost threw my manager out of the meeting. This trial balloon is absolutely vital to your success.

This gives you an opportunity to verify that what you are to propose is exactly what your prospect and his team want. If not, this is a great time to find out and make the changes that he wants in order to present a perfect proposal.

Once you have talked about it a couple of times with your prospect, and you feel that you have all of the details worked out, it is time to put the pricing together. I would have some idea as to the overall range of the project. Then you call and confirm that there are no more changes to the project. If your prospect confirms that everyone is on board with the general scope of the project and the timeline proposed, let your prospect know that you are finishing up the pricing and that it will be in the $xxx,xxx range. This should generate some feedback from your prospect as to what he is expecting in the way of pricing.

Also, send them a copy of a blank contract. This gives them an opportunity to review your agreement and ask any questions prior to the day you are there to make your presentation and sign the contracts. They may need someone like legal to review the contracts, so you want to get this done now so that it does not delay your signing.

If he says that sounds about right, you are good to go. Make sure that your actual pricing comes out a little less than your estimate. Prospects like that. If he has a problem with the price, ask him about where he thought you would be. Assuming he is not off by 30% or more, tell him you will see what you can do. Try to find a way to reprice to get down close to his estimate. It does not have to be exact. If you call him back and tell him that you basically took all of the profit out of the job without removing any of the key items, the prospect will typically be ok with that if you get close.

If he is more than 30% off, you probably will have to ask him what items in the project could be delayed until Phase 2 so that you can get the price in line with his estimate. There are typically a couple of things that you may have thought important but that he does not care that much about.

Run your reprice and call him back. Confirm any thing that you pushed into Phase 2 and that you are now in the same price area as him. This is your trial balloon. You now know what has to be in the project and at what price for your prospect to buy. The prospect has also confirmed these same thing.

KEY POINT: THERE SHOULD BE NO SURPRISES WHEN YOU DELIVER YOUR PROPOSAL.

Section 3: Proposals
Chapter 12 – Review Timeline

In *Glengarry Glen Ross*, Alec Baldwin's character says ABC – Always Be Closing. We have been low key for the last week or so, just talking with our prospect to confirm all of the parts, pieces, and pricing of the project. We may have had a high profile site visit to our best reference, but even then we are letting our prospect talk with our customer to cement the trust in our ability to perform at the highest level for our customers.

Now is the time to make the deal. Each part of the proposal is designed to get us agreement and one step closer to making this deal happen.

We start with the timeline. This talks about all of the steps that got us to this meeting as well as proposed dates to get the agreement approved, any legal or other approvals needed, equipment ordering time estimate, installation timeframe, as well as a general timeline of subsequent phases.

We are going to ask our prospect if this timeline meets his needs and wants. Of course, today and the commitment to move forward with our company is on this list. You walk him through the timeline and then ask him, "Does this timeline work within your needs?" The answer could be yes or it could be that he needs to look through the proposal first. That is fine. Then we ask him, "Assuming that you are comfortable with everything in this proposal, does the timeline work for you?"

It is important that we get a yes at every point in the presentation. We are building to an assumptive yes to do business with your company. I must mention here that this entire sales process is based upon the assumptive close. This closing style requires some confidence on the part of the sales rep. This is not the easiest closing style, but I believe that it is the most effective and has the highest closing rate. I have been using this style for years and have consistently closed 95% of the business I have proposed. Also, if you have done each step thoroughly along the way, there is no reason that you would not get the deal. You are just summarizing areas that your prospect has already approved previously.

KEY POINT: START GETTING "YES" FROM YOUR PROSPECT FOR EACH AREA WE ARE COVERING IN THE PROPOSAL.

Chapter 13 – Review Needs and Wants

By now, you are probably getting tired of reviewing all of the needs and wants. You have done this a number of times with your prospect, however, we need to do it one more time.

There may be people in the room that have not had major roles in the process up to this point. They are the influencers that were not involved in the day-to-day activities that brought us here today. This just gives us another opportunity to ensure that we have addressed all of the areas that your prospect would like to address. It also reminds your prospect, including your sponsor, influencers, and decision makers that they do have significant needs and wants. This also demonstrates how hard you have worked to address those needs. Include any supplemental information, including maps, building layouts, IT structure, anything that you have regarding your prospect.

KEY POINT: GAIN ACCEPTANCE REGARDING ALL OF THE INFORMATION THAT HAS BEEN PRESENTED TO YOU. THIS IS NOT NEW INFORMATION, BUT IT BRINGS EVERYONE TO THE SAME POINT BEFORE WE MOVE FORWARD.

Chapter 14 – Match Services with Needs and Wants

So now we have agreed on what needs to be addressed and the timeline needed to address their needs and wants. Now it is time to overlay each of the products and services that we intend to provide to integrate the solutions needed for this prospect.

This part of the proposal typically takes the most time. You are going through piece by piece exactly how you are going to take care of their needs and their wants. Much of this presentation may be done by the technical members of your team. You may want to introduce each area, but you will want to have your operational experts explain the details of how this is going to work and how it is going to improve the operation of your prospect's business. This should be accompanied by technical cut sheets, drawings, or whatever literature you have to serve as the backbone of your presentation.

Up until now, most of what you have been talking with your prospect about has been theory with a bit of engineering mixed in. They have seen how you have accomplished these tasks with your other customers, and now you are showing them how you are going to do this for them.

Showing is much more powerful than telling, so this part of the presentation must be customized to their situation so that you can accurately explain exactly how this is going to work. Again, be prepared for questions from your sponsor, influencers, and decision makers. At this point, they are realizing that it is the last opportunity to ask questions before they make a decision. Even though they have approved everything along the way, and there are no lurking surprises, they are just becoming aware of how much work you have put into this project and that this train is moving down the track toward a long-term agreement and partnership between the two organizations.

Again, there are no surprises here, but everyone at your prospect's organization needs to get the answers to their questions and those of any other individuals that they need to be able to explain this process to.

Take your time fielding these questions and letting your operations team members interact answering questions. This is when you will probably start fielding any remaining IT infrastructure questions. Hopefully, your operations manager has already spent time with their IT manager to ensure that these details have been worked out. If so, the decision maker will probably ask for a positive nod from IT that we are good to go.

If every step was done correctly and thoroughly, you will survive this part of the presentation without any additional info needed or additional visits necessary. It is vital that all of their questions are answered to their satisfaction before you move on. If not, you will not get this deal until all of their questions have been resolved.

KEY POINT: ALL OPERATIONAL QUESTIONS AND ISSUES NEED TO BE RESOLVED BEFORE THE PROSPECT CAN MOVE TO THE NEXT AREA OF DISCUSSION.

Chapter 15 – Provide Excellent ROI

Not every purchase has a return on investment, but you want to try and find a way to provide your prospect with financial justification for this project. The best way to do this is to quantify the positive aspects of the products and services that you are providing.

If there is an actual financial return such as energy or labor savings, this part is pretty easy. Provide a project with a good ROI, and we can move to the next section of the proposal.

However, if the savings are related to comfort or security or some other means of improvement that is more qualitative than quantitative, you will need to do the best you can. At the least provide them with a list of the benefits that they will receive. Most projects do have some financial reward, but the remainder may be in terms of business equity, branding ability, professionalism in the look of the business, or many other ways that their business is being improved.

There has to be some reward to the prospect in terms of their needs and wants, or there is no reason to take any action. Use your original list of needs and wants, and show how their business will be much better as a result of doing business with you. If at all possible, try to quantify the benefits.

KEY POINT: IT IS EASIER TO GET THE BUSINESS IF YOU CAN IMPROVE THE PROFITS OR REDUCE THE EXPENSES OF THE ORGANIZATION. INTANGIBLE BENEFITS NEED TO BE MADE TANGIBLE.

Chapter 16 – Close by Securing Dates for Installation/Delivery

We have already gone over the timeline, as well as everything else in the proposal. Now it is time to close this deal. Go back to the timeline and say that you just want to check the dates with them one last time.

Will (date) be a good day to deliver equipment? To expedite installation, we will have everything drop shipped directly to you.

Will (date) be a good day to start installation?

As long as we are complete with the project, and at this point we do not anticipate any delays, is it okay if we start your maintenance services on (date)?

Okay, as we cannot control the shipper, the weather, or any other unforeseen delays, as long as we are complete by (date), we should be fine as far as meeting your expectations?

Great! I will put all of these on our project management schedule as soon as I return to the office.

KEY POINT: GETTING APPROVAL ON INSTALLATION DATES CONFIRMS COMMITMENT FROM BOTH PARTIES, INCLUDING ALL OF THE PROSPECT'S STAKEHOLDERS.

Chapter 17 – Sign Contracts

Take out the contracts, sign them, and hand them to your sponsor. Don't say anything. Nothing. Don't cough or sneeze. Make absolutely no noises until they are done signing. They will probably read some or all of the contract. Answer if they have any questions. Otherwise, wait till they are done and say thank you. Then assure them that you will get the agreements entered into your system today and get them on the calendar for installation. That's all, just sign them and shut up like you do this ten times a day. You have done everything to get to this point, this should feel somewhat anticlimactic. They have already reviewed blank contracts, so there should not be any major problems.

Thank them and shake their hand. Put all of your stuff in your bag, tell them that you will follow up with them in a couple of days, and leave.

KEY POINT: SIGNING THE CONTRACT SHOULD BE A MINOR PART OF THE PROCESS. IF YOU HAVE DONE EVERYTHING CORRECTLY, THIS JUST FLOWS AS THE NEXT LOGICAL STEP.

Section 4: After the Sale

Chapter 18 – Push for Quick Installation/Delivery

As soon as the job is booked into your order entry system, set up a meeting with your manager and the operations management team. It is vital that everyone is aware of the visibility of this new customer and the potential for long-term substantial business.

Obviously, it takes some time to get equipment to the jobsite and get started. It is important that this equipment get ordered in a timely manner to ensure that there is not a large gap in time between the signing of the contract and the beginning of installation. During discussions with the customer, it is typically acceptable to propose a two to three week window before installation will begin. You want to be proactive to ensure that it does not become a five, six, or seven week window.

The arrival of equipment and technicians on the jobsite are the first real operational interaction that your customer will have with your operations team. Your future business depends on this being a good relationship. Hopefully, your operations management team has been part of the team that brought in this business, so the contacts and beginning of relationships between your ops team and your customer's team have already begun. That does not mean that you can book the job and move on. You must continue to be diligent in your efforts to start the operations process out in a timely manner and with a smooth transition from you as lead person to your operations manager as the lead with the customer.

Everything up to this point as been about what you can do for your customer as well as what you have done for other customers. Now your ability to get future business is dependent upon what you do for this customer. Starting on time is the first step to that future business, and you need to ensure that this happens if you want to use all of the time and effort you put into this customer to build an annual annuity of business.

Chapter 19 – Be Present with Customer to Showcase Services

While it is probably not your job to install the equipment or start the services, it is your job to continue to prepare for Phase 2 and beyond with this customer. The first task is to ensure that the installation is done correctly. Many times operations teams decide on a "better" way to do things. This typically means cheaper or easier. Unfortunately, that is not what you agreed upon with your customer or your operations team.

You don't have to stop in every day, but you do need to be there at least once or twice a week, and definitely on the big days, the days where there is a lot of activity or a major portion of the project is coming online. If for no other reason, you want to catch a mistake before your customer.

An example of this is a new customer with a lot of repeat potential had purchased a camera system that was quite expensive to overlook their lobby so that they could see all of the activity of their customers and staff as they move throughout the lobby and transact business at the main counter. Unfortunately, the technician, who was actually a former kitchen manager at Hooter's who had quit his job because he did not like it but was hired by one of our contractors whose owner liked to hang out at Hooter's, installed the camera facing the corner. Nobody asked me what the camera was supposed to look at, and I was not there to tell him what it was supposed to look at, and I did not have time to tell our operations manager who would tell our contractor who would tell his technician where to hang each camera on a multi-site contractor.

Well, I found out about this when the customer called me and told me that he had a great view of the corner of the room. Seems like a good expense of over $3,000 by the customer for this camera. Unfortunately, when the customer explained this to the technician, his supervisor, and our operations manager, they did not seem to understand what the customer was saying. After I got a call from my customer, I went to the jobsite and looked at the camera. Of course, it was facing the wall. When I asked the technician about it, he told me that he could not turn it around because it would hit a corner piece that was sticking out. When I asked him if he could move it so that we could see the room instead of the corner, he just looked at me funny.

Throughout the next few weeks, it became humorous to my customer that they could only see the corner even though every day they checked it and asked everyone that they talked to if it could be moved. While the customer got a big laugh out of its installation and seeming inability to move it, they also realized that they needed to check all of our work as it became more and more obvious that the actual technicians were not employed by our company but were anybody that the contractor could drag off the street for that day.

Since our operations manager had given the contractor a contract and some drawings, it was not our job to monitor the installation. So basically, it was up to the customer to monitor the installation. Can anybody else see what is wrong with this picture? I stepped in and basically became the eyes and ears of the customer so that they would not fully realize the extent of our lack of involvement in their project. Now, this took enormous amounts of my time, but which is more valuable, spending time with an existing customer that eventually spent another $550,000 with us or knocking on doors to find a new customer.   As long as you get that repeat business, it is worth your time, but if you do not, you may have just managed your way out of a job due to the low amounts left in your prospect funnel. Now, hopefully you have other repeat customers that do not require as much of your time that can fill your funnel while you are overseeing this installation.

    Another installation that happened to me was a major building renovation early in my career in the education field. Within education, all of the superintendents and business managers know each other well, as they move between districts often and have purchasing consortiums to get lower prices on what they buy. This means that they talk with each other often, so your reputation will definitely proceed you.

    In this case, I had sold one of my first jobs in this industry, at a school district where I had a sponsor and some decision makers that I knew personally. This means that not only was my professional reputation on the line, but so was my personal one.

What happened was in an effort to save money, our branch manager and office manager decided to mount dummy thermostats on the walls in all of the classrooms throughout the district, saving tens of thousands of dollars in wiring and programming costs. They just figured that they would run the buildings from a central computer. Not only was this a poor way to regulate the temperatures in the classrooms, it was also a direct breach of our contract with the school district.

I found out when I got a call from the school's maintenance supervisor. I immediately went to the customer's site and confirmed that we had tried to deceive him and the school district. I notified our management team that the customer was aware of this issue. It was eventually done correctly, but I had already made the decision that I needed to find a new place to sell.

KEY POINT: WHEN YOU CAN NO LONGER LOOK YOUR PROSPECT IN THE EYE AND TELL HIM YOU ARE THE BEST COMPANY IN THE BUSINESS, IT IS TIME TO GO WORK FOR THE COMPANY THAT IS THE BEST. (In my case, I started my own company and successfully competed against my old employer for more than a decade.)

Chapter 20 – Thank Your Customer for the Business and Start Discussions for Phase 2

Hopefully, you have found any shortfalls in the installation and shown your customer all of the good things your organization has done for him throughout the installation.

Now, once the installation is complete, and the ongoing services have started, take the time to buy your customer lunch and tell them thank you. Now I know that a lot of sales people take customers golfing and to major sporting events, but I have never gotten an order for any of those things. I have taken current customers to events, but as ethical concerns have grown throughout business, I now stick to buying my customer lunch once in a while, if they are able to accept that. Some of my customers insist or are required to pay for their own. That is fine.

I highly recommend meeting with your customer over lunch or breakfast at the end of the project just to make sure that there are absolutely no loose ends that need tied up. It also makes for a nice transition point for them to begin being a service customer of your company.

If may be premature at this meeting to ask about the timeline for the next project, but don't be surprised if your customer brings it up. It is almost a natural progression for them. They have been meeting and working with you for months now, and it is just natural for them to bring up their thoughts on Phase 2.

If they don't bring it up, you may want to meet with them again in a couple of months to see how everything is going and talk about the timeline for Phase 2. For a number of my customers, we met like this every year to talk about the work that they wanted to complete that year. As a result, I typically only worked with 2-4 prospects/customers at any one time. If each of them is supplying you with half your quota for the year, that will keep you plenty busy. Even if half of the projects don't close this year, you should always make your quota. If four of them close, you are #1 or #2 in your company every year, and you don't have to knock on too many doors throughout the year, even though it is a lot of funny on a warm sunny day.

Section 5: Additional activities
Chapter 21 – Branding

Branding is today's way of saying reputation. You build a reputation throughout your career with your customers. You also build a reputation with colleagues and others at your workplace, but for our purposes, we are talking about building a reputation with your prospects and customers. I would also include contractors, as they have significant interactions with your customers as well.

How does branding support your work? It gives others an impression of who you are and what you are about. How you act at work and in other social situations determines your brand.

Throughout my career, I typically did not work directly with CEO's on my projects. My typical sponsor was a business manager, one or two steps below the CEO. So, I tried to drive a car that would be similar to my customers. I have never had a Mercedes. When I was in construction, I drove a Ford Explorer so that I could take equipment to jobsites to help with installations and be able to drive onto sites that did not yet have paved parking. When I first started out, I drove a nice Honda Accord that was efficient, sturdy, and good for a family car. Within the last fifteen years or so, I have had a Lexus. I like their dependability, and yet they are still somewhat understated.

    These vehicles indicated a level of success that was consistent with my career, my customers, and the size of projects that I was managing. I also tried to dress with some success, always overdressing a little bit at work, typically wearing a suit and tie even though most sales people no longer where a jacket and tie. I have always told those reps, "You don't ask a guy for $1,000,000 wearing jeans and a tee shirt". I dress to show respect for my customers as well as confidence in what I do. I am serious about my business, and I want to convey that to my customers. I am not suggesting that you go out and buy a new car and clothing, but I am suggesting that you may need to slowly improve your look. If you want to do business in the C-suite, dress like you belong there.

I have always tried to be professional in my social experiences as well. I have coached sports for my kids as well as belonged to some social organizations, including a country club and business club. Through these experiences, I have met people that have gone on to become some of my best customers. Now, I am not passing out business cards at these events, but as you get to know people, they inevitably ask you what you do, and you do the same.

I always try to guide my business to my acquaintances, and over time, they will guide business to you as well. The biggest customer that I ever had started with a conversation while my neighbor and I were taking out the trash. He knew a little bit about what I did, and he told me that his organization had a problem and asked me whether that was the type of work that we do. A couple of million dollars later, our organizations had a ten-year business partnership. Always act as if your customer is watching you – they might actually be watching you.

How you act throughout the prospect phase of your relationship through your ongoing personal and professional phase of your relationship over the years builds your brand. There was a period of time when regardless of what I needed, I could call the person at the highest level in providing that service throughout Northeastern Ohio. Also, my contacts knew me as the go to guy for commercial HVAC and energy savings solutions throughout the area.

KEY POINT: BRANDING IS NOT A BUZZWORD – IT IS YOUR REPUTATION IN THE COMMUNITY AND INDUSTRY WHERE YOU LIVE AND WORK.

Chapter 22 – Networking

Networking is part of branding. Networking should become something that you do without even thinking about it. Whenever you interact with someone, try to think about what you can do for this person. Don't think about what they can do for you, think about what you can do for them. This is the essence of networking. It's about building relationships when you do not need anything. You just do nice or helpful things for others. Eventually this will come back to you when this person is looking to do business. People like to do business with people that they like. People like people that are nice and do things for them.

Look for ways to interact with decision makers. The best way to do that is to volunteer. Get involved in as many social interactions with people that you would like to do business. Don't underestimate any social situation. You never know who knows who or needs what.

Always be positive and look for ways to help. Look for ways to make things work as opposed to stating why they cannot work. People want to do business with positive people that find ways to make things work out. That's networking, plain and simple.

Chapter 23 – Social Media

Be careful how much emphasis you place on social media. First there were beepers, which gave us the ability to get each other's attention during the day. Then cellphones gave us the ability to communicate instantly. Then came email with its ability to communicate 24 hours a day. Each of these improved our work potential and ability to serve our customers.

The advent of social media has changed the dynamic of communication. I like facebook and Instagram if I want to get some information on someone, especially if it is someone I never met. An integral part of sales is the ability to read people quickly and accurately. Social media gives us a view into what they want the world to see and know about them.

I would be very hesitant to utilize social media platforms as my vehicle to get business. First of all, they are not true networking or relationship building vehicles. They allow for people to show you who they would like to be.

Facebook is already diminishing in use among younger adults and teens, giving us a signal that this may not be a reliable method of advertising in the future. Twitter is designed for quick bursts of information. This may be helpful, but again, I would just use these platforms as secondary methods of networking and advertising at best. I would employ other methods of networking and prospecting with the assumption that I will not receive any business through social media, as it is not consistent and reliable.

There is one area of social media that I think can be very helpful to you. This is LinkedIn. This gives you a reliable platform to showcase you personally and professionally, as well as advertise your business for free. Again, this should not be your primary means of prospecting, but it is probably worth a little time once a week or so.

Even more importantly, this is a great way to prospect for business. You can search a business that you want to prospect, and in many cases, get profiles of the potential decision makers and sponsors, eliminating the need to contact a business cold. I have not utilized everything that LinkedIn can provide as I was wrapping up my business ventures as LinkedIn was really expanding into all aspects of business.

KEY POINT: LINKEDIN IS YOUR BEST OPPORTUNITY TO USE SOCIAL MEDIA TO BUILD YOUR BUSINESS. UTILIZE AS MANY OF ITS FEATURES AS ARE APPLICABLE TO YOUR PROSPECTING.

Conclusion

It is quite possible to have a successful sales career without ever employing any of the strategies or tactics discussed in these chapters. You may be in the right industry at the right time, or you may be lucky enough to have a large client that continually buys from you without a lot of effort on your part, or maybe you are successful just because you work hard.

My first mentor told me that it is better to work smart than work hard. Now, I may agree with that statement, but over the years, I have grown in my appreciation for those that work hard. They may be outshined in some years by those who work smarter but not as hard, however, over a career, those that work hard will probably have the most longevity, especially in staying with one company. They may not win awards each year, but they will probably be consistent year to year.

The best bet is to work smart and hard. That is what this book tries to give you – the tools to work smart and hard. If you do both, your opportunities will multiply and your chances for success will also rise exponentially. It has worked for me throughout my career, regardless of where I was working or what I was selling. I am confident that it will do the same for you.

Good luck and happy selling!

Jeff

www.ingramcontent.com/pod-product-compliance
Lightning Source LLC
Chambersburg PA
CBHW071029240526
45469CB00006BD/2151